Anonymous

Souvenir of Petoskey and Bay View

Anonymous

Souvenir of Petoskey and Bay View

ISBN/EAN: 9783337808396

Printed in Europe, USA, Canada, Australia, Japan

Cover: Foto ©ninafisch / pixelio.de

More available books at **www.hansebooks.com**

SOUVENIR OF

PETOSKEY AND BAY VIEW

HALF TONE
ILLUSTRATIONS
FROM
PHOTOGRAPHS

ACCOMPANIED BY

A Short History and Points of Interest
to Visitors.

PUBLISHED BY J. C. VAN NESS, DETROIT, MICH.

PETOSKEY,

"THE PEARL OF THE NORTH," as it has been aptly called, derives its name from old Ne-yas Pe-tos-e-ga, the original owner of the land. He is commonly spoken of as "Chief Petoskey," and many of his descendants still reside in the vicinity. The name, which was Anglicised into Ignatius Petoskey, means the break of day, when the sun touches the hill tops. It is very appropriate; for since it was first started twenty years ago, Petoskey has always been "up and dressed." It is on the G. R. & I. road, thirty-five miles south of Mackinaw City, and is the northern terminus of the C. & W. M. It is situated on the south shore of Little Traverse Bay, a beautiful sheet of water, bounded on the east by a semi-circle of silvery beach, backed by forest-topped sand dunes, and broadening gradually as its shores sweep westward some fifteen miles to the open expanse of Lake Michigan.

From the deck of an approaching steamer the city presents a striking appearance. The arc lights, which range from the water's edge to the crests of the encircling hills, two hundred and seventy feet above, gleam and flash through the darkness—a coronet of diamonds on the brow of night - and furnish a beacon for vessels far out upon the lake. By day one sees the main part of the town spread out upon the sides of a vast natural amphitheater in such a manner that its broad streets, parks and regular squares can be traced as though it were a map. As the tourist draws nearer he sees tall spires rising above the trees, handsome residences occupying every commanding point, and substantial business blocks attesting the thrift and prosperity of the place. The water front, instead of being the unsightly blemish which it is in most cities, is a clean gravelly beach, the favorite resort of tourists watching with eager eyes for the coral and agates cast up by the restless waves. Immediately in front is a park, with flowers and fountains. At the left a precipitous limestone cliff overhangs the railroad that winds along its base, and at the right Bear River hurries down the narrow gorge it has worn through the hills, turning the wheels of a dozen busy factories, and still fretting and murmuring over its work as it tumbles into the blue waters of the bay.

Boulevarded streets, flanked by well-kept lawns in front of comfortable and attractive homes, rise from the beach so gradually that the visitor does not realize the elevation until he reaches the semi-circular crest which separates the manufacturing district from the principal business and residence portion of the town. Then, filling his lungs with the pure and bracing air, washed by its sweep across the waters, he turns his delighted eyes upon the beautiful city, the bay far below, its blue expanse flecked by dashes of white, the land-locked harbor on the opposite shore, the far-reaching wooded hills beyond, and out upon the broad bosom of Lake Michigan, where, forty miles away, Beaver Islands are distinctly seen, floating upon the hazy horizon.

Petoskey sunsets are among the special attractions of this famous resort. Nearly every evening in July and August upon the broad verandas of the hotels, and the porches and piazzas of boarding houses and private residences, hundreds of people sit watching the wide, watery, luminous west. Nowhere are such responsive skies. The shifting shades of crimson and orange and blue mount to the very zenith and play across the heavens like a borealis arch. A hundred windows burst into flame as the sun drops from behind a low lying cloud and sinks into the water—a glowing ball of fire. Silhoutted against the setting sun appears a distant sail, and row boats fleck the glowing path of gold that shimmers on the waves. Then the shadows deepen, the colors fade, the stars blossom "in the infinite meadows of heaven," and the purple twilight is laid like a benediction upon the bending hills.

Among points of interest to visitors at Petoskey are the Indian scalping ground, where prisoners were tortured to death centuries ago, and Marquette's trail, the path trod by the pious missionary over two hundred years since on his way to and from L'Arbre Croche. An artesian well of magnetic mineral water has such remarkable medicinal properties that the principal object of many yearly visitors is to drink the water and take the baths in the large mineral bath house. The Western Hay Fever Association of the United States, composed of "exiles" at different resorts, has its headquarters at Petoskey.

Although it has important commercial and manufacturing interests, it is as a summer resort that Petoskey is best known. A driving park is provided for horsemen, and a recreation park is the scene of frequent base ball, foot ball, tennis and bicycle contests. Fishermen, wheelmen, oarsmen and yachtsmen all have rare opportunities for their favorite amusement, while dress balls and informal hops, and the lectures of the Bay View assembly, furnish constant entertainment for people of all sorts of tastes. The multitude of side trips and excursions to places of interest and neighboring resorts make Petoskey a natural center, and a newspaper devoted to summer visitors, *"The Daily Resorter,"* publishes the news, personals and arrivals of the whole resort region every morning.

Petoskey is deservedly proud of its many excellent hotels, which, together with dozens of boarding houses, cater to all classes, from those of most expensive tastes to the most economical. The city has a complete sewerage system, and pure water is supplied from deep artesian wells by a splendid system of water works. The streets and parks are lighted with arc lights, and the business places and a large proportion of residences with incandescent electric lights. In short, Petoskey has all the up-to-date conveniences, the dummy trains taking the place of street cars. The town was started in 1874, on the opening up of the G. R. & I. railroad. Its unrivalled attractions and advantages caused it to grow rapidly, and it was incorporated as a village in '79 and became a city in '95. In the character of its schools and churches and fraternal, social, literary and musical societies, Petoskey is far ahead of most cities of three times its size. This is because its desirability as a home has caused many people of wealth and refinement to leave their homes in large cities and enjoy well earned rest and comfort in the most beautiful city on the lakes.

BAY VIEW

Is exclusively a summer city, all its four or five hundred cottages being closed during the winter. It was founded as a Methodist State Camp Ground, the first meeting being held August 1st, 1876, with 150 people in attendance.

It soon outstripped the fondest expectations of its founders, and, although annual camp meetings are still held, they have been over-shadowed by the phenomenal growth of that western Chautauqua, the Bay View Assembly, and the equally rapid progress of the Bay View Summer University. The Assembly program covers several weeks and includes the best talent in lectures, concerts, dramatic readings and intellectual entertainments, and the University offers splendid opportunities for receiving special instructions by the most competent instructors in music, literature, elocution, science and art.

The land consists of about four hundred acres, beautifully wooded with natural forest trees, and laid out with the best landscape engineering skill. The cottages and villas of Bay View are situated upon a succession of natural terraces, reaching from the mile of gravelly beach to the forest-crowned summits of lofty hills nearly a mile from the shore. The trees are just thick enough to furnish grateful shade without obstructing the health-giving breezes from the water, or hiding from the people swinging lazily in ham-mocks upon the broad verandas the beautiful vistas of blue water, white sails and distant hills.

But we have already written more than will be read with patience by those who have never visited these famous summer retreats and much more than will be necessary for those who are familiar with their attractions. The photographs reproduced by the engraver's skill in the pages which follow will give a better idea of Petoskey and Bay View than can be conveyed in words.

But after all, there are some things that are beyond the reach of the *fin-de-siecle* photographer and engraver. You cannot press the button and catch the kaleidoscopic changes of the bay. No engraver can represent the rich blending of colors of the emerald setting in which Bay View is gemmed. The most vivid word painter is powerless to reproduce the beautiful pictures in this charming niche of nature's great art gallery.

If you wish to enjoy the beauty and grandeur of the ocean without the repulsive blemishes of the ebb tide; if you would have the clear, pure air of the summit of Mt. Washington brought down to your very door; if you would have the soil of your native land beneath your feet, and at the same time above your head the bluest skies of Italy; if you would float upon the surface of waters so clear that you seem suspended in air; if you would verify the statement of Dr. Brown-Sequard that there is no climate for the invalid like the pure, bracing, health-giving air of northern Michigan –spend your summers at Petoskey and Bay View, the most delightful summer resorts between the two oceans.

VIEWS

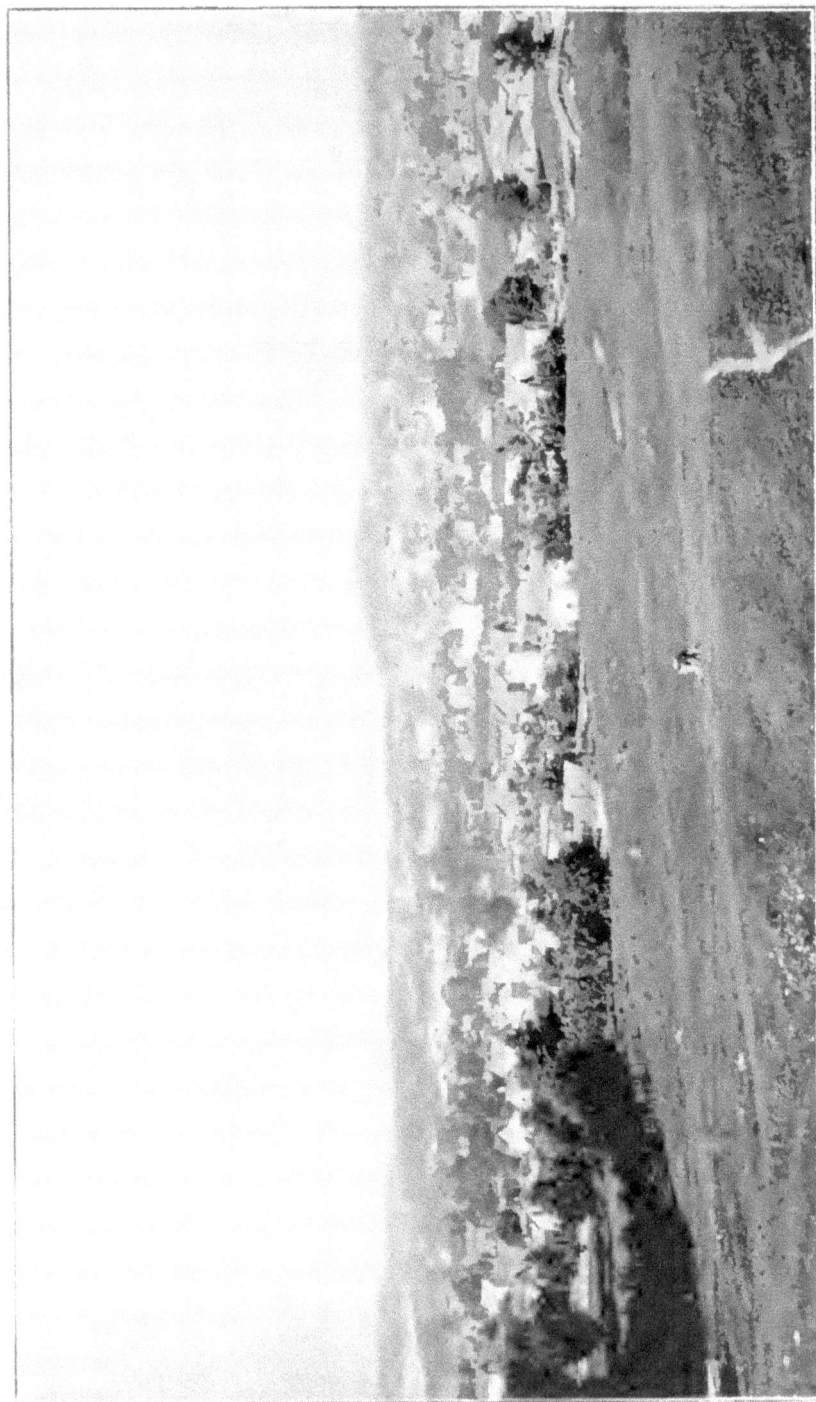

Birds-Eye View of Petoskey from South-West.

Birds-Eye View of Petoskey from South-East.

Birds-Eye View of Petoskey from Howard Street Hill.

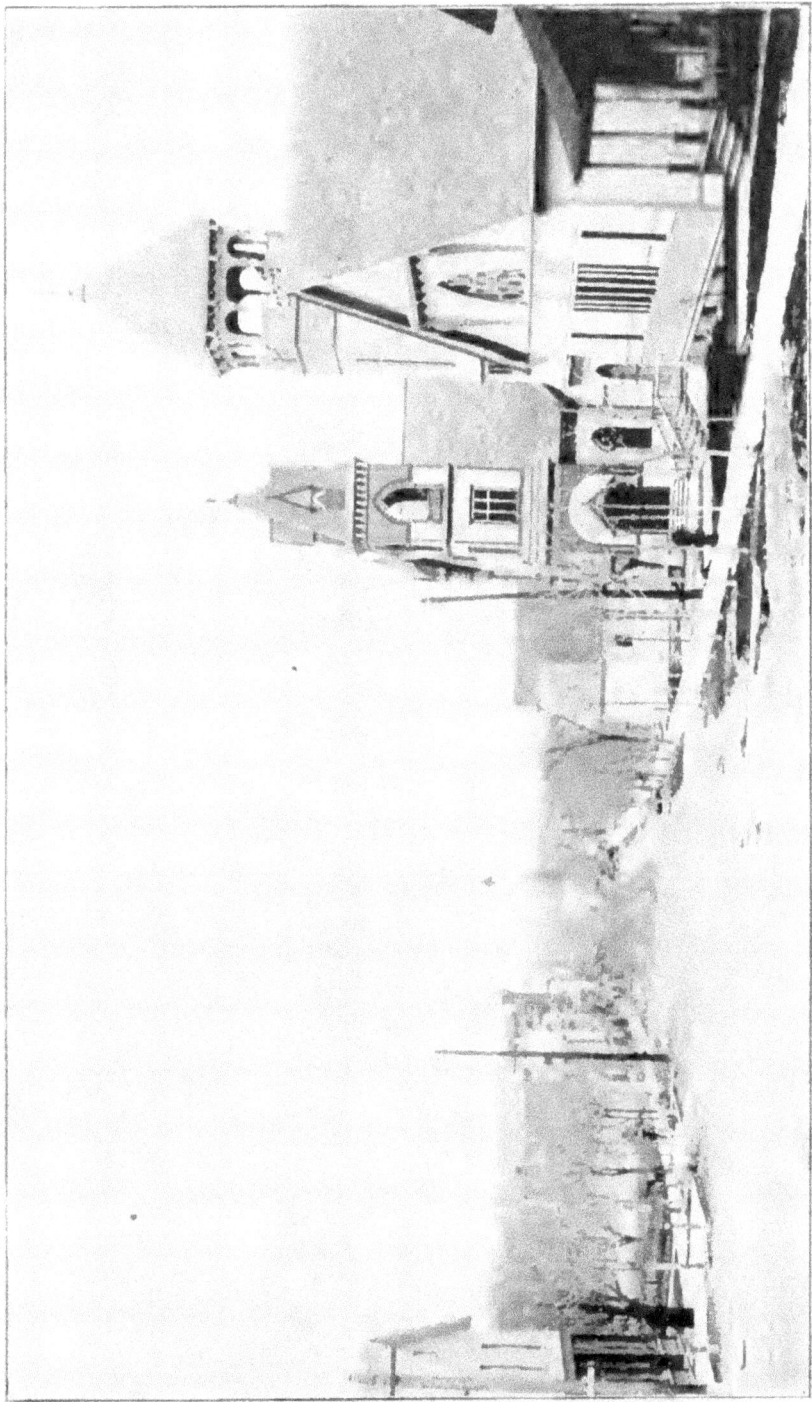

Street Scene, Looking West on Mitchell Street.

Street Scene, Looking North on Howard and Park Streets.

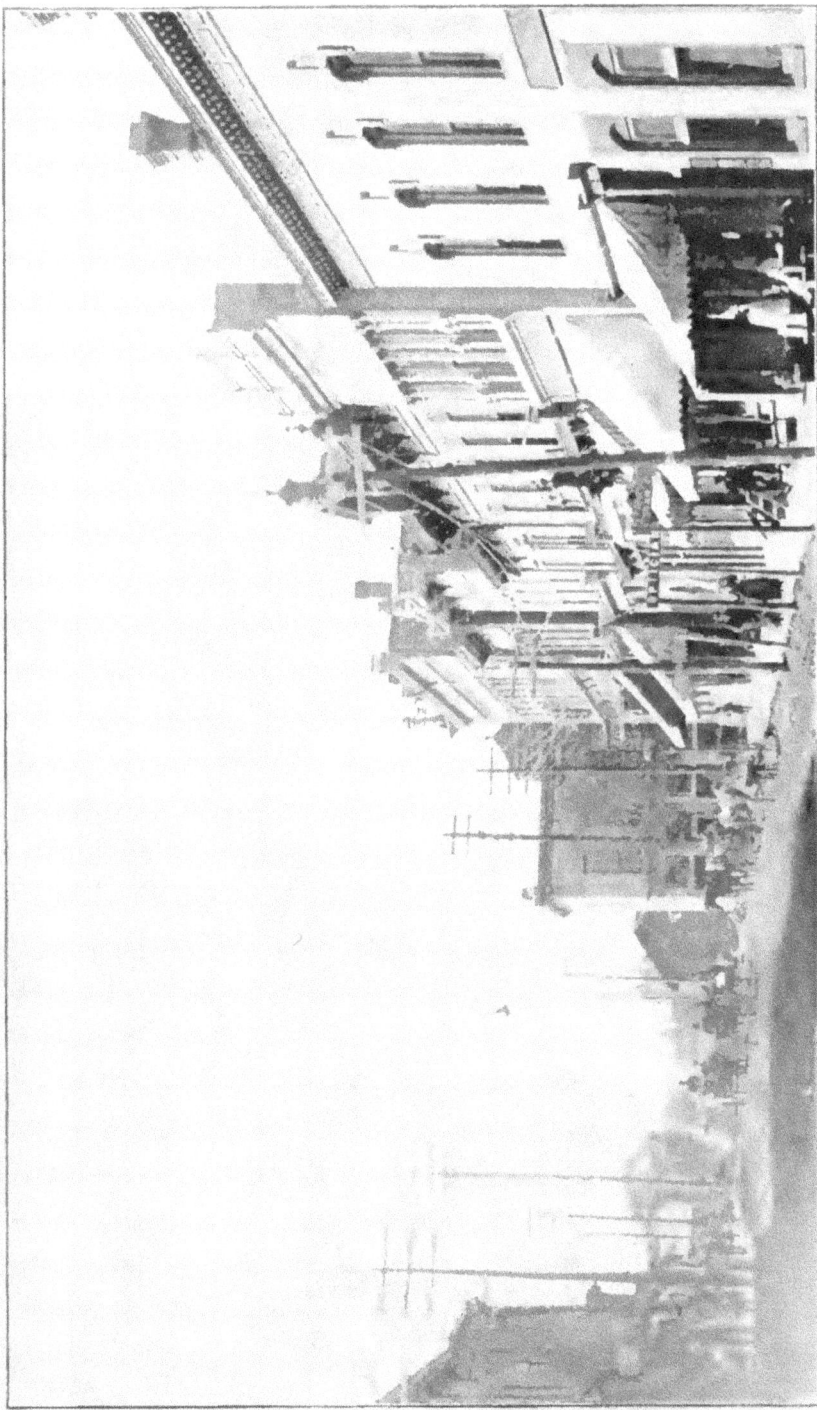

Street scene looking South on Howard Street.

Street Scene, Looking East on Mitchell Street.

Petoskey City Bank Block.

Street Scene. Looking West on Lake Street.

Fisk's Pharmacy Corner, Fochtman Block.

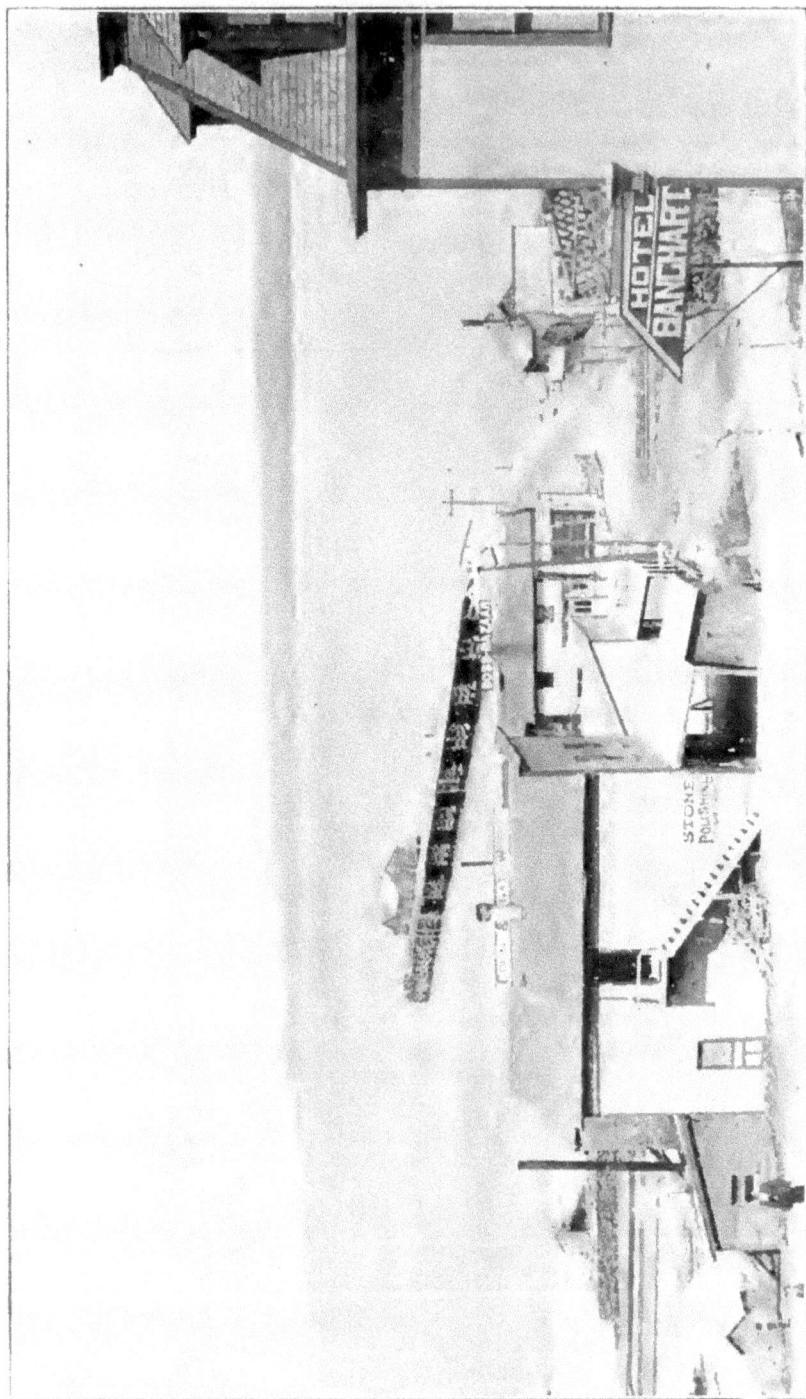

Steamboat Landing and Agate Shops.

High School Building.

Rustic Cottage in Park.

... Arlington Hotel. ...

Residence of W. L. McManus.

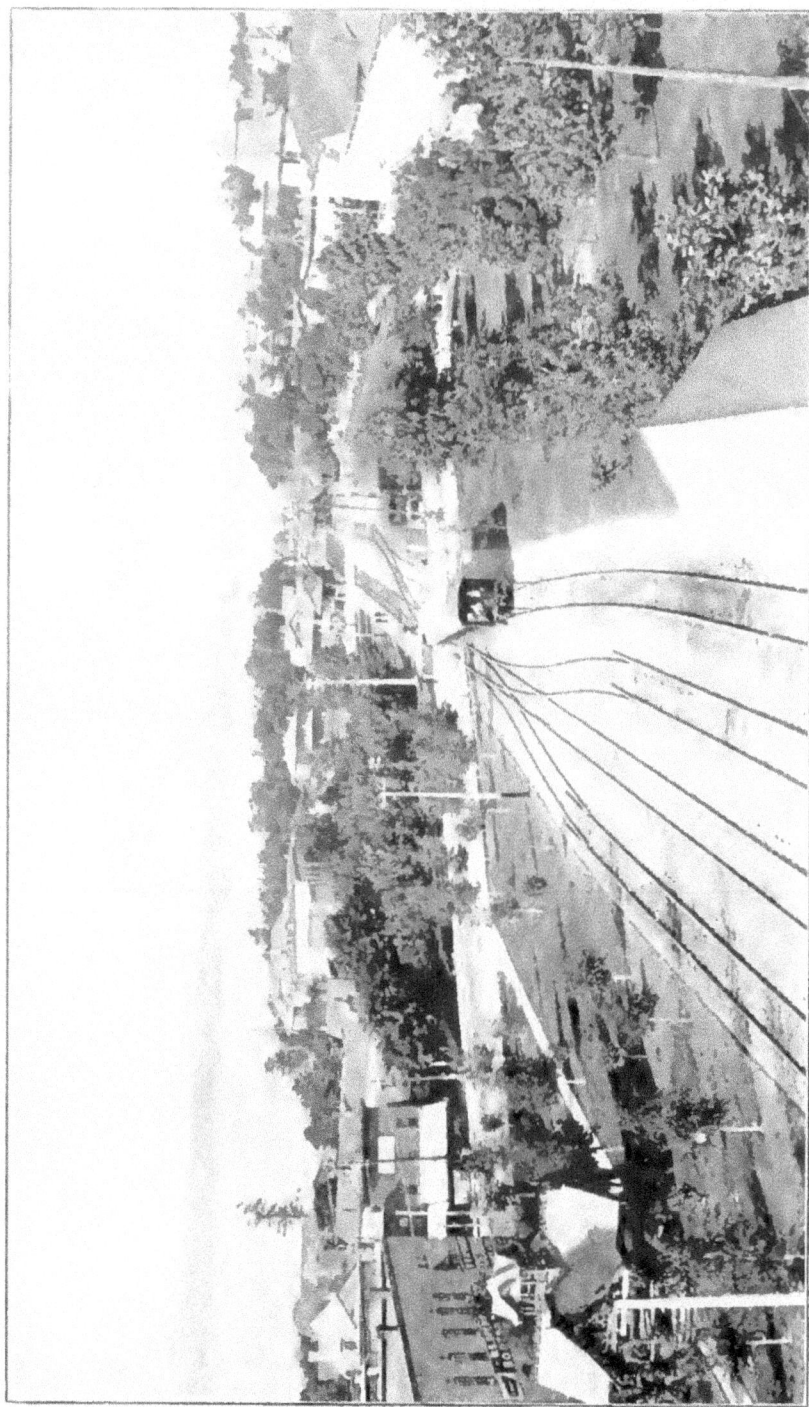

View in the G. R. & I. R. R. Park.

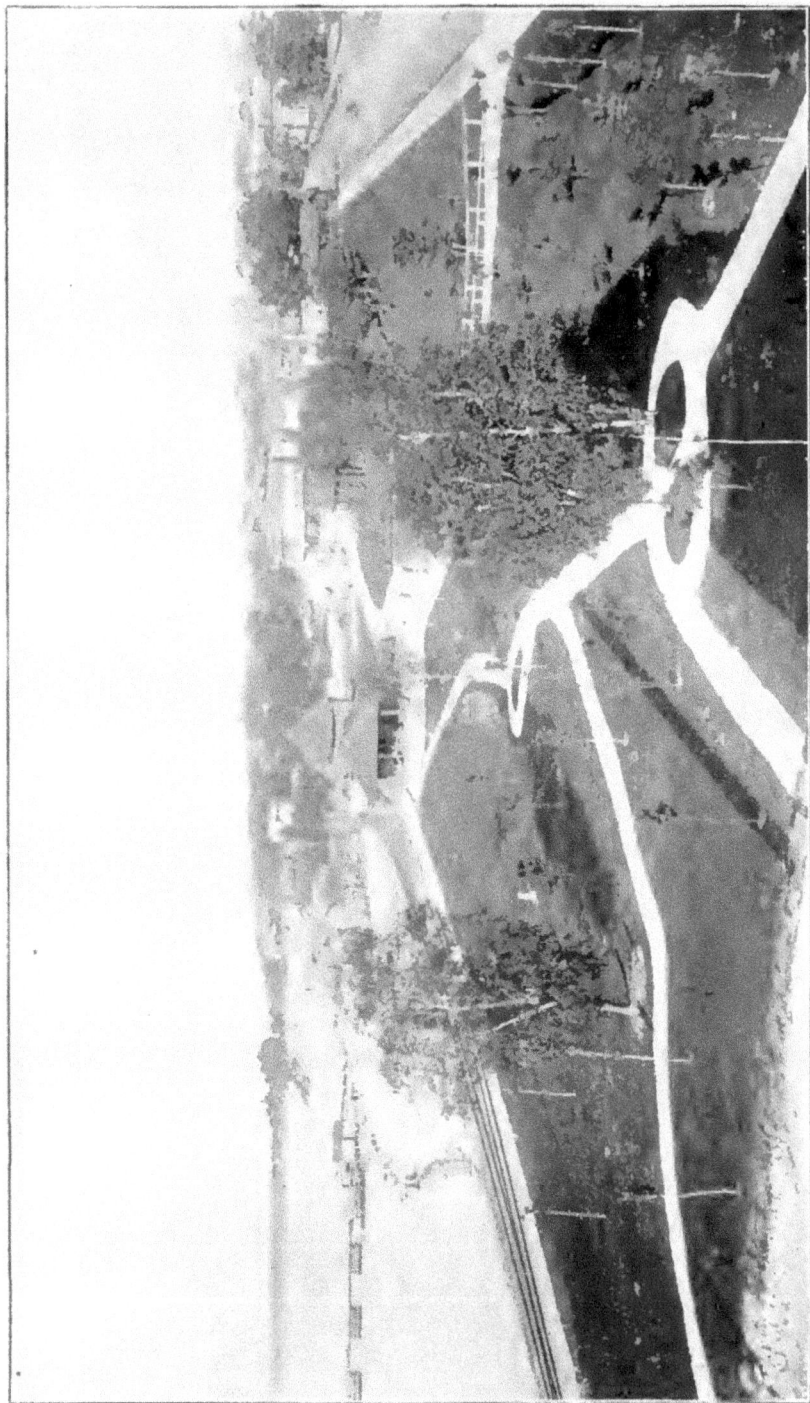

View in the C. & W. M. Railway Park.

Residence of C. W. Caskey.

Excursion Steamer Thomas Friant.

··· Methodist Church. ···

Advent Church.

Presbyterian Church.

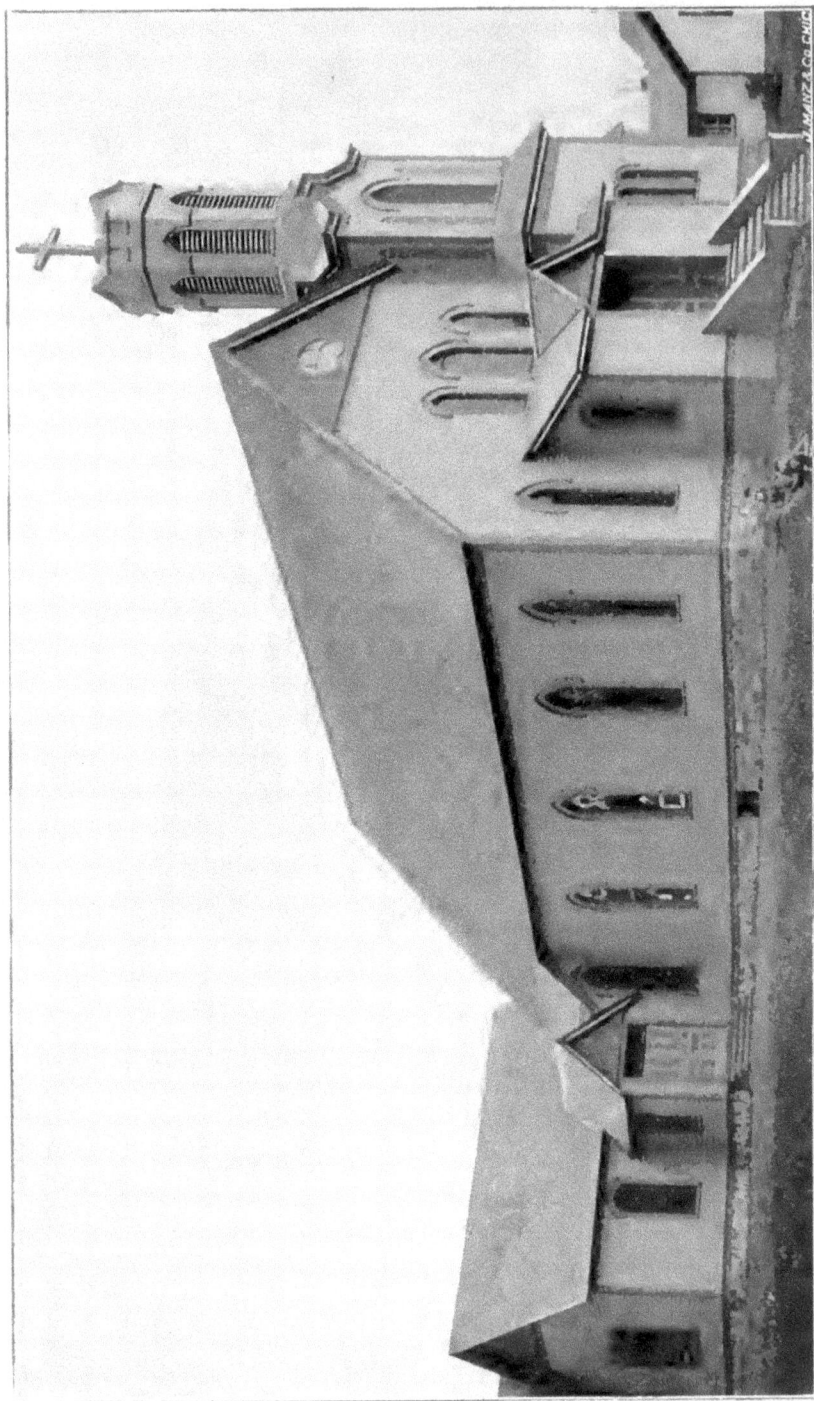

Episcopal Church.

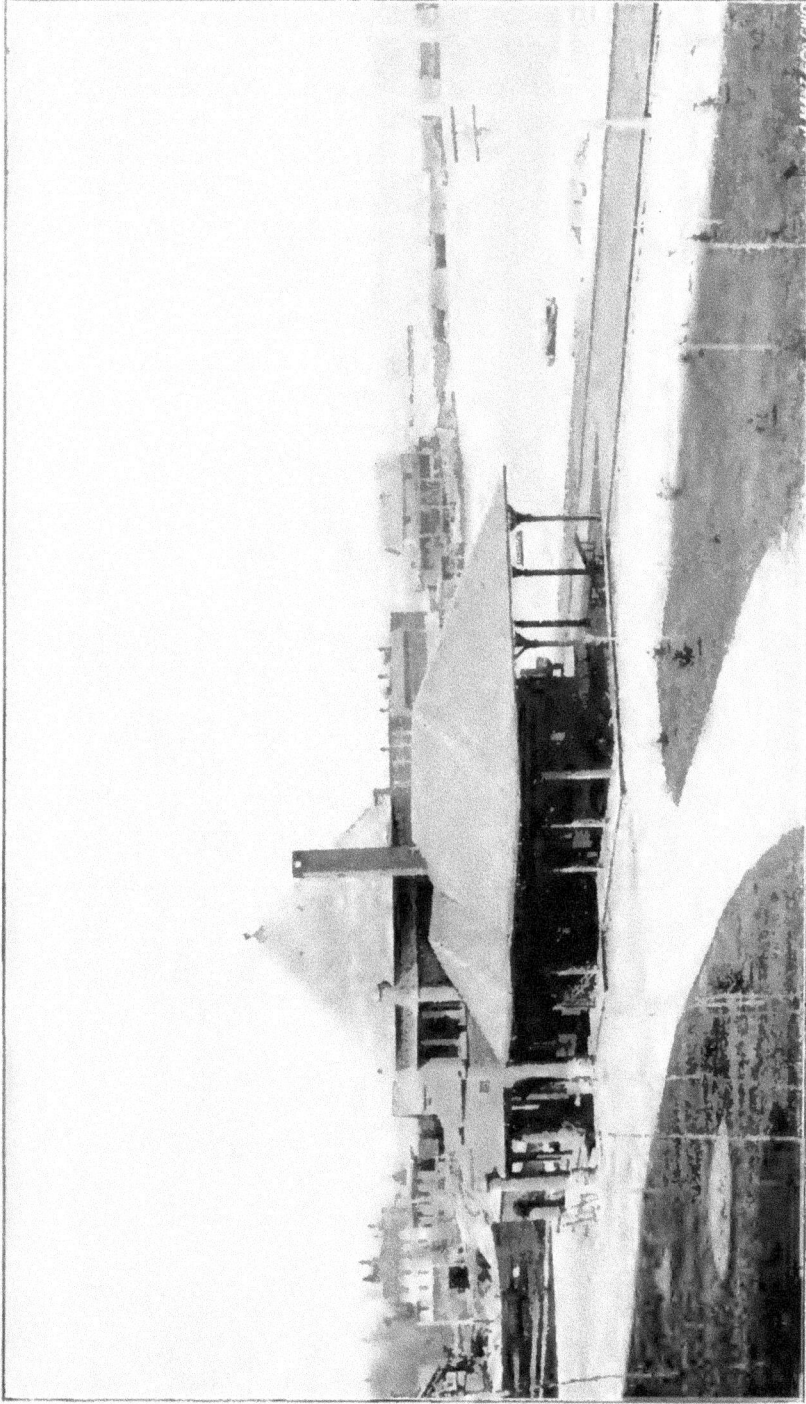

Chicago & West Michigan Ry. Depot.

Grand Rapids & Indiana R. R. Depot.

Steam Ferry Adrienne.

Arlington Spring.

A Rough Day.

The Beach at Bay View.

One of the Terraces at Bay View.

Evelyn Hall, Bay View—W. C. T. U. Headquarters.

Hitchcock Hall. Bay View.

Loud Hall, Bay View.

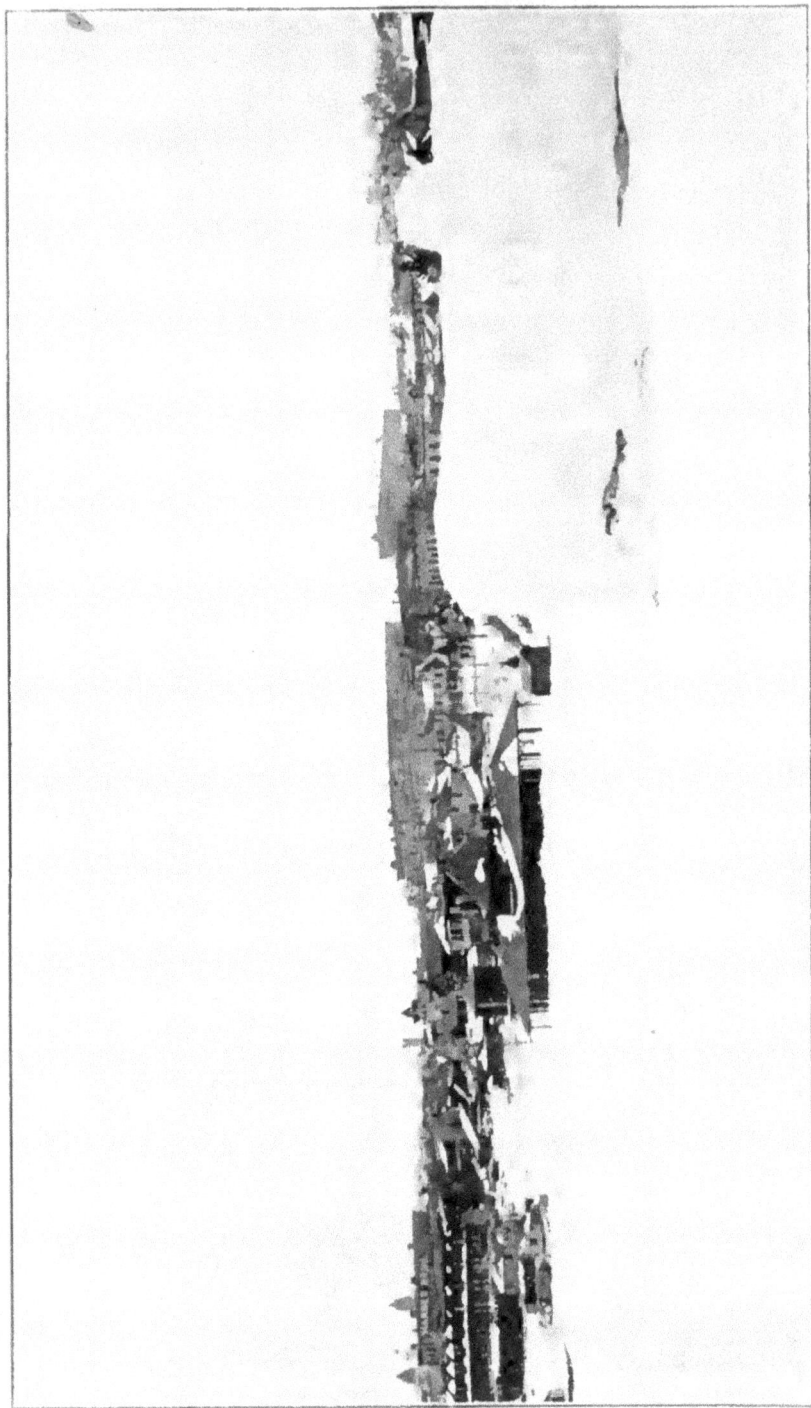

Petoskey from the Bay, in Winter.

City Water Works

S. Rosenthal's Dry Goods Store.

The Famous Artesian Well.

Levinson's Sheriff Sale Fair

Residence of J. H. Levinson.

A Very Artistic Store.

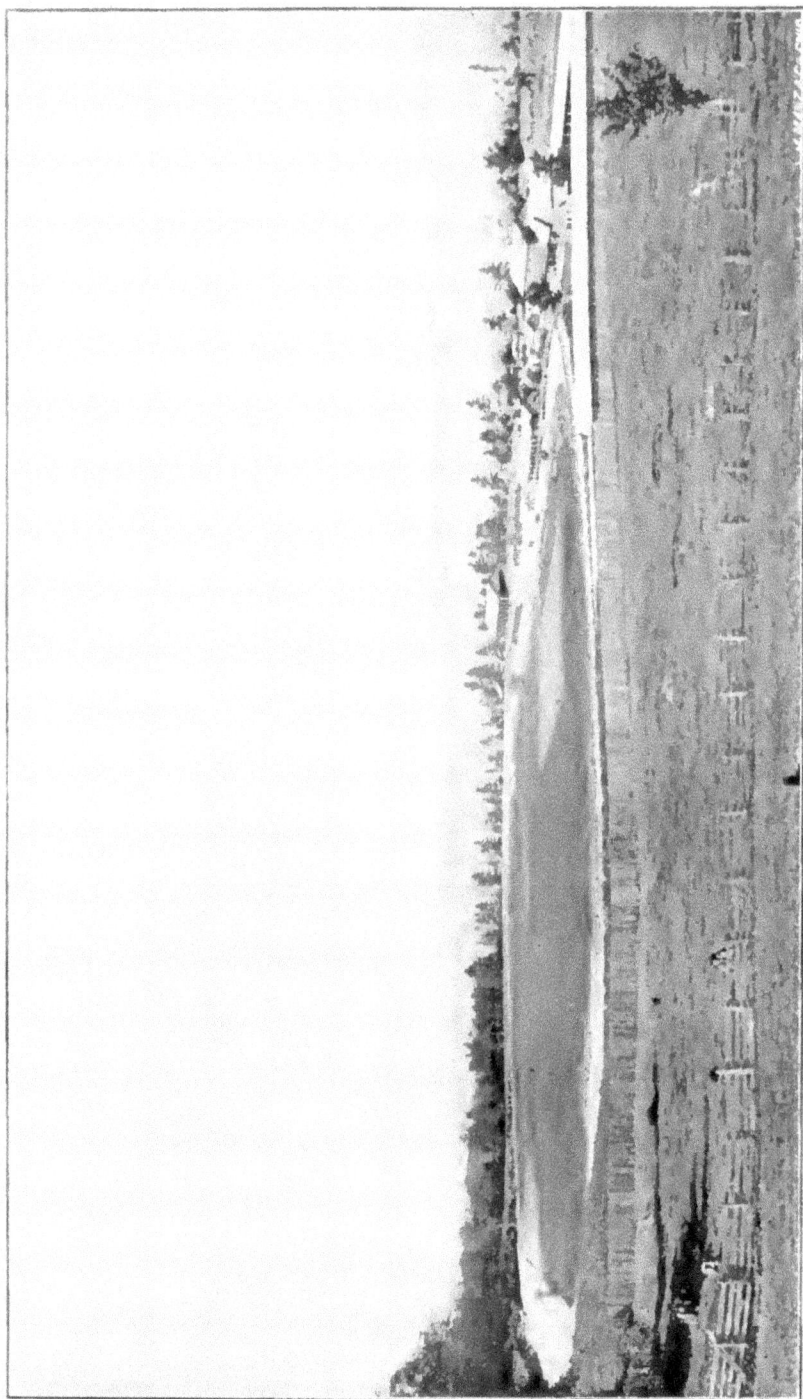

Fair Grounds and Race Track.

Harbor Springs Boat Landing.   Roaring Brook.

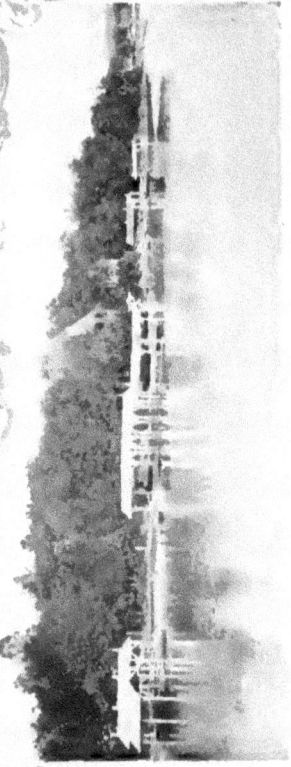

Boat Houses at Harbor Point.

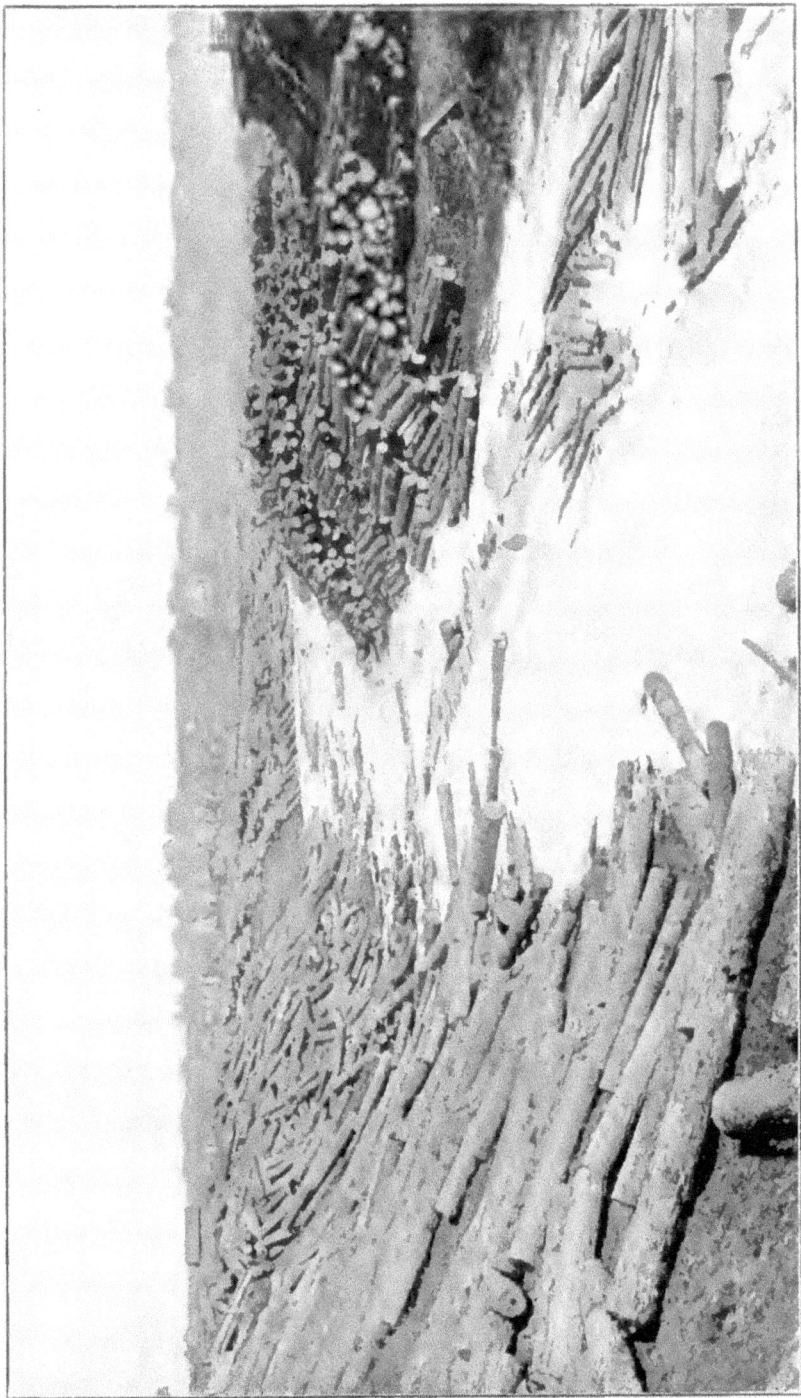

One of the Industries on Bear Creek.

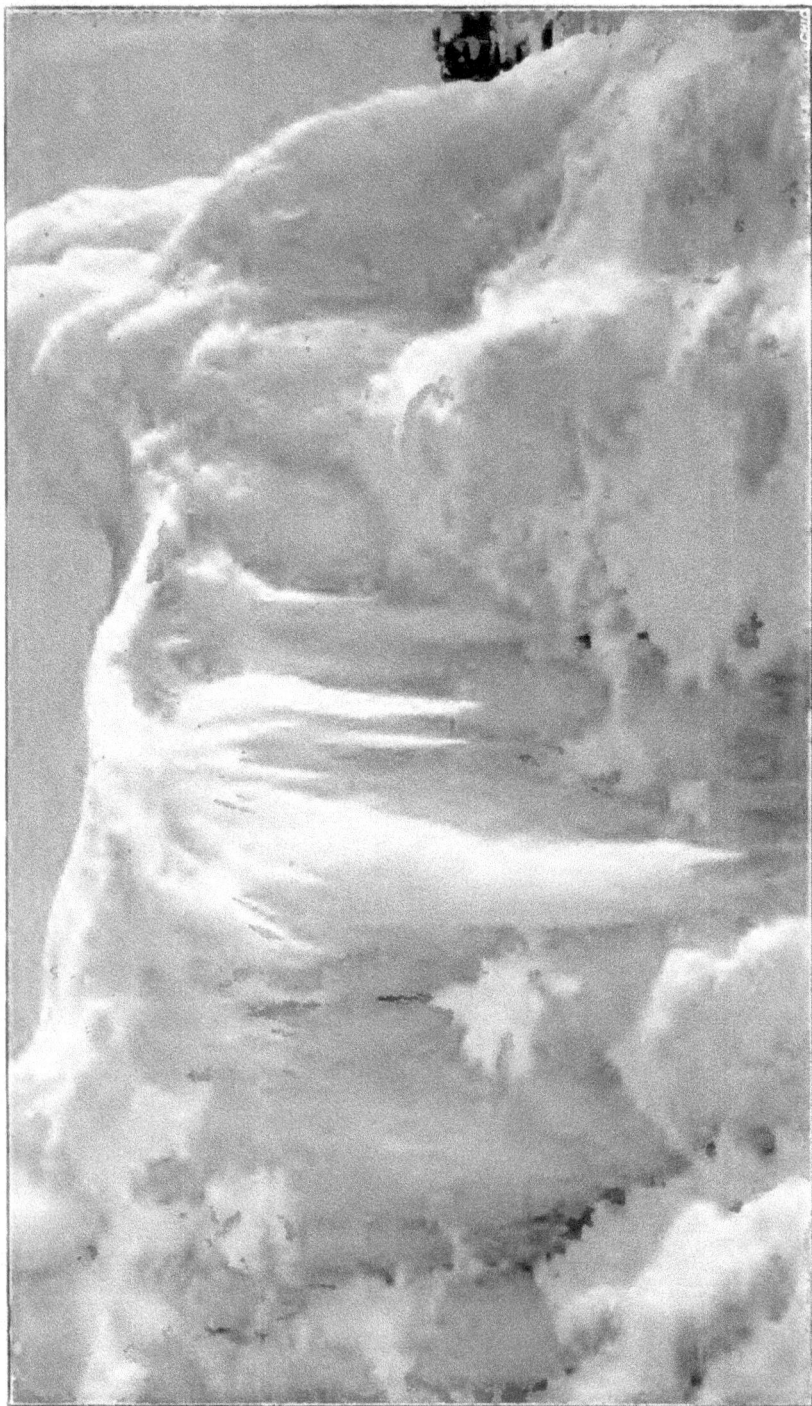

Winter Scene. End of Pier.

www.ingramcontent.com/pod-product-compliance
Lightning Source LLC
Chambersburg PA
CBHW031808090426
42739CB00008B/1209